SCRIPTURAL BASIS FOR MARIAN DOCTRINE AND DEVOTION

Questions and Answers

Rev. John H. Hampsch, C.M.F.

PUBLISHING COMPANY
P.O. Box 42028 • Santa Barbara, CA 93140-2028
(805) 957-4893 • (800) 647-9882 • Fax (805) 957-1631

A woman's-lib speaker proposed a rhetorical question, "Where would man be today if it were not for women?" A disgruntled man at the back of the hall answered, "He'd be back in the Garden of Eden eating strawberries or anything but apples!"

It's true that the first sin was committed by a woman, as Paul reminds us in 1 Timothy 2:14, but he also reminds us in Romans 5:12 that it was the sin of a man as the first human that contaminated the entire human race, including Eve. Eve incited Adam to sin, but Adam's sin caused Eve to lose the state of innocence, together with her posterity yet to come, Adam could say to Eve, "Your counsel caused me to sin," but Eve could say to Adam, "Your sin caused me to lose my primordial innocence," since Adam's original sin contaminated her and the entire human race.

For this double failure by disobedience on the part of our protoparents, God designed a double healing by obedience: one from the "New Adam," by his obedience to his Father in undergoing the redemptive act to satisfy for all mankind's subsequent sin, and one from the sinless "New Eve," by her obediential consent to bring the Redeemer into the world. As Eve was closely associated with the "Fall", without causing it, so Mary was closely associated with the Redemption, without causing it. This magnificent design of God for salvation history has put the Virgin Mary in a most unique position among all creatures in his creation.

Mary's influence through the centuries has been incalculable, not just as the person most frequently portrayed in the history of art, but also in literature, for she is the one about whom more has been written than any other human after Jesus, with entire libraries devoted exclusively to Mariology in many locations around the world. Her modern influence extends even to such mundane matters as the parking policy in New York City, as when *The New York Times* had a front-page notice stating, "Because of the Feast of the Immaculate Conception, alternate-side parking is suspended in New York City today. Other rules remain intact."

If Mary had not existed, or had not given her *"fiat,"* the second Person of the Trinity, the Word, would not have taken flesh, and Jesus Christ as the God-man would not have existed. There would then have been no Messiah, no redeemer, no redemption, no Christianity, no Church with Christian denominations, no Christian schools, hospitals, or orphanages; no papacy, no priesthood, no Eucharist, no Christian forms of prayer, no church buildings, pews, altars, etc.; no Christian missionaries, no counting of dates from the birth of Christ (A.D.), no calendars with the current year listed, no car models designated as this specific year's model, etc. Countless other situations would exist that we can't even begin to imagine if Mary had never existed.

In view of all this, it seems worth considering her sublime status. One way to do this might be to pose a few questions and objections about the Mother of Jesus, and to answer them primarily within the framework of Sacred Scripture, on which authentic Mariology must be ultimately based.

What is the purpose of devotion to Mary or to any of the saints?

ANSWER: It is threefold, as Vatican II pointed out (L.G., art. 51):

1) To imitate the good example of their life (1 Cor. 11:1).

2) To enjoy fellowship in the "communion of saints," i.e., the believers in heaven and on earth (Eph. 3:15; Heb. 12:1).

3) To seek their intercessory prayer for our needs in body, mind, and spirit (see 2 Mac. 15:12-16; Ps. 106:23).

Why pray to Mary or to any saint?

ANSWER: We should not pray *to* Mary or *to* any saint or angel, in the strict theological meaning of the phrase "pray to," for one may pray only *to* God. But we pray *with* angels and saints, and they pray *with* and *for* us. In the broader sense, we can say that we "pray to" Mary and other saints or angels by addressing them prayerfully, asking them to pray *for us*, as we do in the Hail Mary: "Pray for us sinners, " (to God, of course) while we pray for ourselves in tandem with her prayers for us. Thus, praying "to" any saint is exactly like asking a friend on earth to pray for us or to pray with us, as Paul "prayed" that his fellow Christians would pray for him (1 Thes. 5:25; Eph. 6:19, etc.) and as Epaphras did (Col. 4:12), and Paul himself prayed for others (Eph. 3:16; Col. 1.3). Saints in God's presence have more prayer-power than we do, for they are not as faith-limited as we are; hence, they're excellent prayer-partners for us.

Must we go to God through Mary? Didn't Jesus say "Come to Me"? The Bible says Jesus is the only mediator between God and man.

ANSWER: You are correct in stating that the Bible names Jesus as the only mediator between God and humans (1 Tim.

2:5; Acts 4:12; Heb. 7:25). However, in each of these citations, as the context shows, it refers to him as *redemptive* mediator (Savior or Redeemer). Mary's mediatorship is *non-redemptive*; it is only petitionary (impetratory) mediatorship, just as our own mediatorship would be if you prayed to God for me at my request. No Scripture passage states that Jesus is the only intercessor as *prayer mediator* — although he is the greatest one (Heb. 7:25; 9:24; Rom. 8:34; Is. 53:12; I John 2:1), and the one through whom all prayer must *ultimately* pass to reach the Father (John 14:6).

Vatican II states (L.G., art. 62) that no creature, even Mary, can be put on the level of Jesus, the only Redeemer. However, just as Jesus' singular eternal priesthood is shared by both his ministers and the laity in various ways (I Pet. 2:5), and as his one goodness is radiated among creatures in various ways (I Tim. 4:4), so also his unique mediatorship does not exclude but rather gives rise to a manifold shared mediation, in petitionary form, within which Mary's is pre-eminent.

It was this petitionary mediation that Paul requested of the Ephesians, asking them to "pray for all the saints (believers)" and he "prayed" for them to pray for himself (Eph. 6:18-19; 1 Th. 5:25), while he himself prayed for others (Eph. 3:16; Col. 1:3), as did Epaphras (Col. 4:12). Mary's intercessory power with Jesus is of the same type as that of St. Paul and Epaphras, and the same as yours or mine, namely petitionary. But as the "highly favored one—full of grace" (Luke 1:28), hers is far more powerful, as evidenced by her successful intercession for the embarrassed host at the Cana wedding, persuading Jesus to work his first miracle, even "before his planned time" (John 2:4).

Mary in heaven is not deprived of that intercessory power that she exercised on earth, since heaven is not a place of deprivation, but fulfillment, as implied in Hebrews 11:40. Even in the Old Testament we find examples of deceased persons (Jeremiah and Onias) prayerfully interceding for the living (II

Mc. 15:12-16). Those in heaven have more prayer power than they had on earth, for they are not faith-limited in heaven, since they see God directly (Job 19:26; 1 Cor. 13:12; 1 John 3:2).

This type of mediatorship or intercession is mentioned many times in both Old and New Testaments; for instance, 1 Kings 13:6; Ps. 106:23; Eph. 1:16, etc. Judas Maccabeus saw a vision of Onias, the deceased holy High Priest, praying for the Jewish nation. He was accompanied by a vision of Jeremiah offering prayers for the Jews and for Jerusalem (2 Mac. 15: 12-16). But even when others on earth or in heaven pray for us, their prayers still are channeled through the ultimate mediator, Jesus: "No one comes to the Father except through me" (Jn. 14:6).

Our reliance on the talents and gifts of others here on earth reflects our interdependence in sharing the benefits of God's gifts with his people. Likewise, we can share in the benefits of the saints' gifts, including their intercessory power.

Thus, graces given to Mary were meant to benefit us. And as they were given to her in a *special* degree — implied in Luke 1:28, 42, 48 — she can be said to intercede for us in a way that is particular to her. Hence her preeminence as an intercessor, even though the nature of her intercession is the same as that which we exercise, though far greater in power because of this status given her ("highly favored one" — "full of grace"). Therefore, not to recognize the favor and blessings God has bestowed on Mary, and her response to them which benefits us, would be to ignore God's economy of grace.

Mary's mediation is not a "relay" system; she does not relay our needs to God as if they go through her to him. Rather, it is like two parallel arrows going Godward, in accord with the biblical promise: "If *two* agree to ask anything . . ." (Matt. 18:19). Mary doesn't stand "between" us and God, to forward our prayers to him, but joins us in a fellowship of prayer.

Why not imitate Christ, as he commanded ("Learn of Me"), rather than Mary, whom we're not commanded to imitate?

ANSWER: Devotion to Mary or the saints, states Vatican II, involved not only depending on them for their intercession, as the Israelites did with Moses (Ps. 106:23), or enjoying their fellowship in the "communion of saints" (i.e. believers in heaven and on earth; Eph. 3:15; Heb. 11:40; 12:1), but also imitating the good example of their life (James 5:10). Marian devotion by way of imitating her virtues will draw us closer to the Lord, whom she herself closely resembles.

Honoring by imitation of virtue does not detract from God, but leads us to him. That's why many Protestant evangelists strive to imitate the prayerfulness and zeal of champions like John Wesley, or Finney, or other great Protestant luminaries. This is part of our fellowship with the saints, living or dead (Eph. 3:15). Hebrews 11 speaks of inspiring examples of faith, and 12:1 speaks of being "surrounded by such a great cloud of witnesses" that should inspire us.

Paul presented himself for imitation in this way, as shown in seven passages inviting us to imitate him as reflecting Christ (I Cor. 11:1; 4:16; 1 Th. 1:6; Phil. 3:17, etc.). Paul's urging of others to imitate him was not an appeal to "distract" his spiritual clients from imitating Christ, but to incite them to a closer imitation of Christ, for he wrote that the very meaning of Christian life is the imitation of Christ and the realization of his life in us (Eph. 5:1-2).

The rationale for Mary's preeminence in this patterning is that she did this better than anyone else; in her Christ's grace has been most truly realized. While Jesus is the perfect Redeemer, Mary is the one most perfectly redeemed—the one in whom Christ's grace is most perfectly realized for she was redeemed from sin *preventatively* not curratively. By imitating her as the paradigm of all those redeemed, we become more like the Redeemer. The brilliance of the full moon is the reflection of the light of the sun, far surpassing the planet's reflection of the sun. In the same way, Mary's virtue reflects God's own virtue better than other saints and angels do. Furthermore, as the moon doesn't "distract" us from the sun, but only reminds us of it, so does Mary remind us of God's goodness reflected in herself as God's most perfect creature. Admiring God's masterpiece is a compliment to the divine Artist. In Mary's own words, "He who is mighty has done great things for me, and holy is *his* name." (Luke 1:49).

Visualize Mary hovering over the crib of Jesus at Bethlehem, or weeping at the foot of the cross. In this meditative stance, do you find that Mary "gets in your way" of approaching Jesus or "distracts" you from him? Doesn't such Mary-involved meditative prayer help you to "focus" on him and love him more? Such prayer fellowship with Mary, or with any saint, can hardly "distract" us from Jesus; rather it reinforces our Christocentric devotion. Mary is always directing us to Jesus, as she did at Cana: "Do whatever *he* tells you" (John 2:5).

Moreover, while it is most praiseworthy to obey Jesus' mandate to imitate him, still, in the spectrum of Christ's majestic splendor there are areas that can't be imitated — for instance, his creatorhood (Heb. 1:2), his status as founder of the Church (Matt. 16:18), his role as head of the Mystical Body (Col. 1:18), his function as Redeemer, etc. Mary provides for us a model of virtue that does not exclude "non-imitable" areas (even her sinlessness we can at least *strive* to imitate).

Since millions of good Christians don't have any devotion to Mary, can it be said to be really necessary to have such a devotion?

ANSWER: The state of the question is misplaced. It is like saying something need not be done this way if it can be done another way; it misses the point entirely. It's like saying that since the Eucharist is not the *only* way God gives grace, we need not participate in the Eucharist. The point is that God has established a plan of salvation, and we profit most when we recognize it and fulfill *all* of his plan. The original question would be better phrased as a double one: Is it "necessary" to cultivate such devotion? The answer is No. Is such devotion in accordance with God's will and plan? The answer is Yes.

To lack Marian devotion is to regard Mary as just another Christian, deserving of no greater veneration than anyone else. This would be a false and unscriptural position, in view of the triple reference to Mary in Luke 1 as "blessed" or most favored. Is it scriptural to refuse to relate to Mary in accordance with the Spirit-inspired word of God that "all generations will call me *blessed*"? With those sacred words in mind, it might be asked, why is it that only those with Marian devotion refer to her as the "*Blessed*" Virgin Mary?

Can't devotion to Mary become distorted by "Marian fanatics," leading to real theological error?

ANSWER: This is possible, but not if the devotion is kept within the parameters of the Church's guidelines, as Vatican II pointed out (L.G., art. 67). The two extremes to be avoided are: first, "false exaggeration by neglecting Mary's dependence on Christ, who was her Savior," as she herself said (Luke 1:47); and second, "too summary an attitude in considering her special dignity." Examples of the first abuse would be to regard Mary as not needing redemption, or to regard her as "Mother of Mercy" in such a way as to make her more merciful than Jesus. An example of the second abuse would be to regard her as just another biblical personage, who happened to be related to Jesus as his mother.

I have a hard time believing in Mary's Immaculate Conception, since the Bible says that "all have sinned" (Rom. 3:23),

which must include Mary. Moreover, she herself spoke of "God my Savior" (Luke 1:47), so she must have needed saving from sin like the rest of us.

ANSWER: Your question is a perceptive one, and one that is often presented by non-Catholics, and sometimes by Catholics unaware of the Church's teaching. The question deserves an unequivocal answer.

First of all, to clear up a possible misconception for some readers, the Immaculate Conception does not refer to the miraculous conception of Jesus in the womb of Mary — the virgin birth; it refers rather to her exemption from original sin from the time of her own conception in the womb of St. Ann. And by extension, it also refers to her preservation from personal sin throughout her life.

There is no doubt that Mary was redeemed or "saved"; yet she was conceived without sin, or immaculate. The solution to this paradox was first formulated by the medieval Franciscan theologian, Duns Scotus — a solution eventually incorporated into the 1854 proclamation of the dogma of the Immaculate Conception. (This proclamation was not a reaction to heresy, but a declaration of a long-held truth finally *defined* after having been *refined* theologically through the centuries.)

Scotus pointed out that just as health can come either by way of prevention of disease or by way of cure of disease, so can salvation — the reception of redemption. Mary was "saved" or redeemed *before* Jesus' redemptive act, by the *anticipatory* application of that redemptive act (in God there is no sequence of time). "In view of the *foreseen* merits of Jesus Christ" (not by her own merits), says the document, Mary was *prevented* from inheriting original sin from the moment of her conception. By her pre-Calvary redemption, it was as if she were "given merchandise before the check was cashed," so to speak.

Also, by the same Christ-earned merits, she was preserved free of any personal sin during her entire life. *She was not saved from sin, but saved from sinning*. This "preservative redemption" was basically the *perfect* redemption, since it involved not the healing of sin, but the preventing of sin. This "perfect redemption" inspired the poet Wordsworth to forthrightly acclaim Mary as "our tainted nature's solitary boast."

Regarding the biblical statement of Romans 3:23, that "all have sinned," two things must be kept in mind: first, the word "all," if taken with absolute literalness, would have to include Christ, which is absurd (see Heb. 4:15); and second, the context of Romans 3:23 (like every reference to the universality of sin) shows an emphasis on the truth that all human beings need redemption (see verse 24). Jesus — the only one who *by his very nature* was sinless, and hence the only one who could redeem us — didn't need redemption, of course. Mary *is included* among all those needing redemption, even though for her it was "preventative" rather than "curative."

Unlike Jesus, "Mary was not sinless *by her own nature*," wrote Pope Pius IX; only by God's grace was she immaculate (unstained by sin). And Mary knew that only God could "create a clean heart" (Ps. 51:10), so she didn't hesitate to acknowledge God as the source of her gifts: "He who is mighty has done great things for me" (Luke 1:49).

Is the doctrine of the Immaculate Conception supported by Scripture?

ANSWER: That question might elicit a threefold answer: First, although there are not *direct* references to the doctrine, neither is there anything in Scripture that denies it, including two citations referred to in the question above. (Of course, this negative response *by itself* is not compelling). Second, there are a number of *indirect* scriptural references to support the doctrine, as explained below. And third, there are eight biblical references to support tradition as a source of divine revelation

— Mary's sinlessness being an *ancient and consistent tradition,* first noted a few years after the death of St. John the Evangelist. (Mary's sinlessness was proclaimed as early as A.D. 370 by St. Ephrem, but implicitly acknowledged as early as A.D. 150).

Such authentic tradition, Vatican II reminds us, is not above Scripture, but "serves" it, helping to interpret it, just as a preacher interprets God's word, "rightly dividing" it (2 Tim. 2:15). The Bible tells us to "hold fast to the *traditions* that have been handed down to you, whether by word of mouth or by writing (2 Tim. 3:14). Other biblical references to tradition as a source of revelation include: 2 Tim 1:13 and 2:2; 2 Thes. 2:14 and 3:6; Jude 3; I John 2:24 and Heb. 2:1. Tradition in this sense is a consistent belief held by the People of God from ancient times. This form of tradition is not merely *human* tradition, such as cultural or unwarranted disciplinary practices like those that Jesus condemned in Mt. 15:3 and 6, Mk. 7:8 and 13, and Paul condemned in Col. 2:8. The Bible states that God-authorized tradition is an acceptable form of revealed truth (serving Scripture, not replacing or dominating it, as Vatican II pointed out).

Let us look at a few of the *indirect* scriptural references to the doctrine of the Immaculate Conception. The Bible affirms that freedom from sin must be God-caused (Ps. 51:10); only by his power could anyone make the claim, "I have been blameless before him and have kept myself from sin" (Ps. 18:23). God speaks of his spotless Bride: "You are wholly beautiful, my love, and without a blemish" (Song of Songs, 4:7). Mary was uniquely predestined to be the Bride of the Holy Spirit, who was to impregnate her (Luke 1:35). She had to have a sinless body to bear the God Incarnate, Jesus, who Paul calls the "Wisdom of God" (I Cor. 1:30), for "Wisdom will never make its way into a crafty soul nor stay in a body that is in debt to sin" (Wis. 1:14).

Furthermore, by bringing God to the human race, Mary became the model of the Church in that same function — a function for which it is called to be "holy and immaculate, without stain" (Eph. 5:27). It was thus appropriate for God to predestine her to pattern this ideal for the Church, by keeping her immaculate or stainless.

To the serpent (Satan) in the Garden of Eden, after the "Fall," God said, "I will put *enmity between you and the woman*, and between your offspring and hers; he will crush your head." (Gen. 3:15). In this passage (called the "proto-evangelium" or "prefigured Gospel") the word "he" refers to the woman's offspring, which in the Hebrew text is a masculine word, logically leading Christian tradition to refer to the woman's offspring as Christ; who else but Christ, by the redemption, would crush the head of the serpent? If this offspring of the woman is Christ, then the "woman" must be Mary, referred to prophetically, not Eve. The prophesied "enmity" between Satan and this woman, Mary, bespeaks an uncompromising opposition between the initiator of *sin*, and a *sinless* woman, who was most highly graced or "full of grace" (Luke 1:28) and therefore sin-free or immaculate; for, since grace displaces sin (Titus 3:7), anyone "full of grace" is totally sinless.

Mary, as the God-assigned "enemy" of Satan would have to be one who had never been under his dominion by either original or personal sin, in order to be maximally worthy to tabernacle in her body the "Offspring" prophesied in Genesis — the sinless God Incarnate — and bring him forth to redeem a sin-filled world.

The prophesied victory of "crushing" the power of Satan would not be a meaningful victory if the conquering Redeemer had assumed his body from a woman who had been subject to the Adversary (which is the very meaning of "Satan"). Christ's victory would have been only a pyrrhic victory if His suffering and glorified Body — the very instrument of the victorious redemption (I Cor. 11:24) — had been drawn from a mother who had been contaminated or "conquered" by his enemy through sin. Christ would not derive his sinless body from a mother's body that had been even slightly sin-contaminated.

Why do Catholics believe that Mary was taken up, body and soul, into heaven? I can find nothing in the Bible to support this.

ANSWER: As in the case of the dogma of the Immaculate Conception, the doctrine of Mary's bodily Assumption into heaven is supported by Scripture, although indirectly, not directly. First, negatively, there is nothing in the Bible that contravenes this doctrine. Secondly, cases of bodily "assumption" into heaven (or "raptures," as some prefer to call them) are mentioned in the Bible, so the phenomenon is not unprecedented; five times the Bible speaks about the "assumption" of either Enoch or Elijah into heaven, body and soul (Gen. 5:24; Jude 14; Heb. 11:5; Sir. 44:16 and 49:16). Thirdly, the belief is based on a strong tradition, traceable back to the A.D. 400's, that Mary was assumed into heaven after her death. The Bible validates tradition itself as a viable form of revelation (see the eight relevant passages cited above, in the answer to the query on the Immaculate Conception). Reinforcing all this in more recent times is the mounting archaeological and paleographic evidence attesting to Mary's Assumption.

Consider the "spiritual assumption" that Paul speaks of in Ephesians 2:5-6: "God brought us to life with Christ — it is through *grace* that you have been saved — and raised us up with him and gave us a place with him in heaven." For Mary, who was "full of grace" (Luke 1:28) and whose sacred body had enwombed the "Holy One," when the Spirit came upon her and the Most High overshadowed her (verse 35), it would have been most appropriate for God to preserve that body from death's corruption, as Christ's was (Ps. 16:10; Acts 13:55, 37), and for her to be bodily lifted to heaven after the fashion of her divine Son in his Ascension.

If this privilege could be extended to Enoch and Elijah, and possibly also to those many who were resurrected in Jerusalem on Good Friday (Matt. 27:52-53), then it would seem inappropriate for Mary, the one "blessed among all women" to be deprived of that same privilege.

Mary's Assumption was a kind of "rapture" that all of us believers will experience some day as the resurrection of the body (I Thes. 4-17; John 11:23-24), although hers was "premature" by comparison. Just as she experienced an anticipatory redemption by her Son in her Immaculate Conception at the beginning of her earthly life, so also at the end of that life it was appropriate for her to experience an anticipatory "rapture" in being "assumed" bodily into heaven by that same Jesus.

Mary's immediate "glorification" by being assumed into heaven in a privilege paralleling Jesus' Ascension was most fitting also by reason of the fact that she was so closely conjoined with him in his suffering in the very act of redemption on Calvary. Thus, in a preeminent way, Paul's words should have been applicable to Mary: "We suffer with him that we may also be glorified with him" (Rom. 8:17).

The ancient traditional belief in Mary's bodily Assumption, as a privileged reflection of her divine Son's Ascension, was made a dogma by Pope Pius XII in 1950. And like the dogma of the Immaculate Conception, it was not promulgated in reaction to heresy, but in confirmation of a centuries-old devotion that has thrived in the Church under the Holy Spirit, who guides the Church "into all truth" (John 16:13).

These are a few of the multifarious insights that the Spirit has delivered to the Church in the gradual Scripture-based development of Mariology through the centuries. The theological insights mentioned here deal with only a few of Mary's privileges.

Let us never weary of praising God, as Mary did, for all she has received from him for us to enjoy and admire. Truly, "He who is mighty has done great things" for *us* by doing such great things for Mary, as "our tainted nature's solitary boast." As part of "all generations" that will call her blessed, let us admire and honor God's splendiferous masterpiece; in doing so we will be implicitly honoring the Divine Artist himself who fashioned her.

No one would deny that Mary was the mother of Jesus. But isn't it wrong to give her the title "Mother of God"? She didn't pre-exist God as a mother pre-exists her offspring; nor did she give rise to the Deity.

ANSWER: Certainly no creature can create (or procreate) the Creator, who is God. And Mary therefore was obviously not mother of the Godhead; she could not have as offspring the eternal Deity. Yet she can be properly called the "Mother of God." The reason for this, simply stated, is that Jesus is a person who is God, and if Mary is the mother of that person, Jesus, she can rightly be called the mother of God, or, as Elizabeth called her, "the mother of my Lord" (Luke 1:43).

This sounds oxymoronic, like "the procreator of the Creator," but it is in reality a paradox or *apparent* contradiction, like many passages in Scripture; for instance, Peter's accusation, "You took the life of the Author of Life" (Acts 3:15), or the fact that the emotional weakness causing a bloody sweat was found in the same Jesus with an omnipotent strength to raise people from the dead or walk on water. The same Jesus that suffered hunger pangs for forty days multiplied bread to feed the hungry. The Jesus who said that the Father was greater than himself (John 14:28) also said that he and the Father were equal (John 5:18).

Such paradoxes can be understood only when the basic tenet of Christology is understood, namely that the one Jesus was both God and man, and that he was referred to in each of these roles separately, as the "Son of God" and the "Son of Man," at different times and in different contexts. With this distinction, we can thus say that in one role he created Mary, and in the other he was procreated by Mary. He produced her, and yet was produced by her.

Since Jesus was one person, both human and divine, we can predicate of him either nature, as shown above in scriptural citations. It can be said that he was a divine person, and as such, the *divine* son of Mary, making her the mother of a divine person, the "Mother of God." She was not the mother of the humanity of Jesus, but the mother of the human person, Jesus; and *she was not the mother of the divinity of Jesus, but the mother of the divine person Jesus.* Motherhood relates to the person of the offspring, not the nature. Your mother is not the mother of your human nature, but of you, the person. If you, as a person, were President, I could say that your mother is the mother of the President. Likewise, if Christ as a person, is God, then Mary is the Mother of God.

The Council of Ephesus in A.D. 431 condemned the heresy of Nestorius, the bishop of Constantinople, because of a false teaching of Mariology based on a false teaching of Christology. Nestorius refused to call Mary the Mother of God because, he claimed, Jesus was two persons, human and divine, rather than *one single person with two natures*, human and divine, (distinct from each other but united in what is called the "hypostatic union"). The Nestorian heresy admitted that Mary was the mother of the human person of Jesus, but denied that there was any mother for the divine person, since a divine person could have no creatural origin. Clumsy disregard of the person-nature distinction thus led to Christological, and hence Mariological, heresy. That same distinction is implicitly ignored in the question presented above.

The Church's earliest teaching, based on Scripture, was that Jesus was one person, fully human (Heb. 2:14, 17) and yet fully divine ("true God": 1 John 5:20; "great God, Jesus Christ": Titus 2:13). As divine, the second Person of the Trinity had no beginning, but an eternal past. Yet as human he had a beginning in time in the womb of Mary, as Paul succinctly states: "at the appointed *time* ... the Son of *God*, born of a woman" (Gal. 4:4). "Christ Jesus, being in the very nature of God ... made himself ... in the very nature of ... human likeness ... as a man" (Phil. 2:5-8). "The Word [the second Person of the Trinity] was made flesh and dwelt among us: (John 1:14) "and the Word was God" (v. 1). From that time of his enfleshment, or Incarnation, he was called Jesus rather than the Word. Yet this same Jesus claimed that he had existed before Abraham (John 8:58), and even before the world (17:5), with the same *personal* identity. All this proves that Jesus is *one person* with two natures, one without a beginning, and one with a beginning.

From all this there originated the doctrine of the "Divine Maternity." It highlights Mary's most basic prerogative, and like all her prerogatives, it is Christocentric. Without this privilege, she would not have the privilege of the Immaculate Conception, or the Assumption, or the virginal conceiving of Jesus (called the Virgin Birth), or her title "Mother of the Church" — that is, Mother of all the People of God.

What is the rationale for assigning to Mary the title of "Mother of the Church" — or of all God's people? Isn't that a bit extravagant? Does it have any scriptural basis?

ANSWER: Acceptance of this aspect of Mary's maternity presupposes an added element — a recognition (at least an implicit recognition) of the fact that Mary's personal and maternal love for Jesus as the Head of his Mystical Body extends to us members of that body as part of Christ himself in some way (Eph. 5:30; Rom. 12:5; I Cor. 12:12).

There's another scriptural basis for the title. John takes note of a pivotal moment that he was privileged to witness on Calvary (John 19:26-27): "Jesus said to his mother, 'Dear woman, here is your son,' and to the beloved disciple, 'Here is your mother.'" The word "woman" had been used in the protoevangelium of Genesis 3:15, referring to the woman whose offspring would crush the power of Satan; and Jesus had addressed Mary as "Woman" at the water-to-wine miracle episode at Cana. Here we see him lovingly using that same form of address on Calvary.

In the Hebrew language, the word translated (via the Greek) as "woman" was not bereft of tenderness (hence it is often translated as "Dear Woman"; it might be likened to our affectionate term, as in phrases like "the little woman and I are going to do thus-and-so." In addressing John, Jesus used the phrase "your mother," but in addressing Mary, he used the title "Woman," not "Mother." The connotation of universalism in the consignment would have been truncated if he had addressed her as "Mother." In addressing Mary as "Woman," Jesus used a more ample title, so as to commission her (implicitly) as a king of "universal woman," one whose nurturing care would reach beyond John to all those redeemed at that very occasion. This is the first subtle intimation of Mary's assignment as "Mother of the Church."

The counterpart assignment spotlighted John's new filiation, the primary beneficiary of Mary's newly extended maternity. But notice that Jesus did not address John by name, thus again deftly "universalizing" the beneficiary of Mary's maternal love and care corporately to all the newly redeemed, for whom John stood as proxy (being the *only* apostle present at that redemptive event). This was the second subtle intimation of Mary's role as "Mother of the Church — the redeemed people of God."

As we can call Washington "the Father of our country," we can call Mary the Mother of the Church. But it is only because she is the Mother of Christ, that Mary can be the Mother of the members of the mystical Body of Christ her Son. Thus again it is seen that this Marian prerogative, like all of them, is derivative of that of her Divine Maternity.

The Divine Maternity undergirds not only all Marian doctrine, but also all Marian devotion, with spiritual implications reaching beyond the doctrinal ones. For instance, by virtue of her Divine Maternity we acknowledge her intercessory role as Mediatrix, in the Hail Mary and rosary prayers: "Holy Mary, *Mother of God*, pray for us sinners..."

I can accept much of Catholic Marian theology, but Marian devotion seems alien to me. While I speak of Mary as "the Virgin" or "the Virgin Mary," I find her devotees referring to her as "Our Blessed Mother" or "Dearest Mother Mary," etc. Such a personalized relationship is not cultivated with other biblical personages like Elijah, or Paul, etc. Isn't such devotion maudlin, or am I perhaps spiritually deprived?

ANSWER: One of the many devotional outgrowths of the basic doctrine of the "Divine Maternity" explained above is the veneration (not worship) of Mary as "*Our* Mother," or (to fulfill the biblical prophecy, "All generations will call me blessed") invoked as "Our *Blessed* Mother." Most non-Catholics (and many marginal Catholics) are not "acculturated" to Marian devotion from early childhood — a devotion is "caught more that taught," like countless other human attitudes and habits, such as family affection, love of classical music, habits of gambling, attitudes about divorce, drugs, etc. Culture plays a role in religion and spirituality, as well as every aspect of life.

To grasp the extent of cultural influence in prayer, try to identify with a devout Muslim at prayer, or a Jew at the Wailing Wall, or a Hindu at a funeral. Likewise, a Marian devotee, trying to explain to a non-devotee the awesome interior love-surges or the exterior phenomena experienced at a Marian shrine, would usually get a disappointing response of calloused indifference. A deep and abiding awareness of Mary as our spiritual mother is one of the most beautiful, comforting, and spiritually uplifting insights that can be given by the Holy Spirit — undoubtedly part of that "spiritual wisdom and understanding" that Paul prayed would be given to the Colossians (Col. 1:9) and Ephesians (Eph. 5:17). Since all authentic Marian devotion is Christocentric, as Vatican II pointed out (*Lumen Gentium*, art. 62), all true Marian devotees have a much richer devotion to Jesus because of it.

One of the greatest rewards of filial Marian devotion this side of heaven is the incalculable *joy* that deep Marian devotion and love will engender. There is joy in honoring Jesus, the Divine Artist, by admiring Mary, his masterpiece; the joy of being, in some way, another Jesus for Mary; the ineffable joy of feeling constantly secure and at peace, because of confidence in her fathomless protective love for us; the joy of experiencing success by her blessing on all our works done for God's glory, as she teaches us to rely on her Divine Son to "make our paths straight . . . and give health to the body" (Prov. 3:6-8); the joy of making her known, loved and served; the joy of seeing her honored by God "who has done mighty things" for her, honored by humans of "all generations that will call her blessed"; the joy of growing in love of Jesus under her tutelage; the joy of bringing happiness to Jesus by honoring Mary, and happiness to Mary by honoring Jesus. The saintly Marianist brother Leonard once wrote: "To give Jesus the delightful joy of loving Mary on earth through me and in me, and to give Mary the joy of seeing her Son live again in me (John 15:5) — what a glorious thought!" Is it true to say that those lacking such joy are missing something in their spiritual life? The question almost answers itself.

I have read Catholic authors who write of Mary as "Co-redemptrix" (co-redeemer) with Christ. Isn't this unbiblical,

since the Bible says clearly in several places that Jesus is the only Savior or Redeemer?

ANSWER: Of course Jesus is the only Savior (Redeemer), as Peter proclaimed explicitly in Acts 4:12: "Salvation is found in no one else, for there is no other name under heaven by which we are saved." This basic doctrine is reiterated in Matthew 1:21; Acts 10:43; John 14:6; 1 Timothy 2:5. Mary can be called a "co-redeemer" (feminine form: "co-redemptrix") only in the most analogous sense — and this in three ways:

1) She shared in the Redemption by consenting, with her *"fiat"* to give the world a Redeemer.

2) She was present at the climatic event of the Redemption on Calvary, and suffered with him by her compassion what he suffered in his passion. With Simeon's prophecy fulfilled as a "sword (of sorrow) pierced her soul" (Luke 2:35) in seeing her Son die a tortured death, she became the "Queen of Martyrs"; in a pre-eminent way she fulfilled the words of Peter by "participating in the sufferings of Christ" (1 Pet. 4:13); or, to use the enigmatic words of Paul, by "filling up what is still lacking in regard to Christ's afflictions, for the sake of his body, which is the church" (Col. 1:24). Mary, in a preeminent way, and we in a lesser way, can all thus be vicarious "redeemers with a small 'r,'" as Bishop Sheen used to express it.

3) She participates even now in the redemption by making the redemptive merits of Christ more applicable to us earthlings by her intercessory prayers for us to *"receive,"* ever more perfectly, Jesus as our Savior (John 1:12). In this respect she's like a soup-kitchen manager, who does not produce or deliver the free food, but merely urges us to "receive" and enjoy the freely available merchandise. Like Paul, she wants to "impart some spiritual gifts" (Rom. 1:11) which were also earned for us as "bonuses" of Calvary's redemptive act (see Rom. 8:32).

If the Virgin Birth has always been a fundamental doctrine of Christianity, why do Mark and John in their Gospels fail to mention it?

ANSWER: Both of those Gospels omit the record of the first thirty years of Jesus' life and deal only with his public life as Messiah. Mark's opening words refer to "Jesus Christ, the Son of God." By describing his Father as divine, not human, he implies the absence of a human father, inferring that his mother must have conceived him virginally. John, in effect does the same, saying, "the Word was made flesh . . . who came from the Father" (1:14).

Why don't any of Paul's epistles mention the Virgin Birth?

ANSWER: Paul's letters were not intended to comprise a complete catalog of Christian doctrine, but were written as informational or correctional letters to specific congregations or persons. Yet all fourteen of his epistles open with a reference to the Father-Son relationship in the God family, such as "God the Father of our Lord Jesus Christ" (Col. 1:3), again implying no earthy father, with the consequent implied conclusion that his mother must have conceived him virginally.

Matthew claims Christ's birth fulfilled the prophecy of Isaiah 7:14 about a virgin giving birth. But is not the word virgin there a mistranslation of the Hebrew word "almah," meaning "young woman"?

ANSWER: The Hebrew word *almah* can be translated "young woman," "girl" or "maiden", as well as "virgin." It presumes rather than states virginity, as in Genesis 24:43, where it describes Rebekah as a "young woman" *before* her marriage to

Isaac, and her virginity is affirmed by verse 16. *Almah* is *never* used to describe a married woman. Isaiah uses the one word which is never applied to anyone but an unmarried woman. This is not true of the alternate word *btula* that can mean virgin only when it is further specified as such. Isaiah had to chose one of the two available terms, neither of which *always* means virgin, he chose one that always *excludes* the connotation of marriage, and hence more exclusively conveys the idea of virginity. The Greek Jewish scholars who translated the Old Testament into the Septuagint Greek version chose the Greek word *parthenos*, which *always* means virgin. Moreover, the Greek New Testament interprets the Hebrew, tying it in with the angel's words to Joseph attesting to Mary's virginity (Matt. 1:20-23). Remember that Matthew had received an inspired understanding of the correct sense of the Hebrew Scriptures, because he was with the apostles when Jesus "opened their minds to understand the scriptures . . . everything written . . . in the prophets" [including Isaiah] (Luke 24:44-45).

I believe in the Virgin Birth, that Mary was a virgin when she conceived Christ. But I can't agreed with the Catholic doctrine of her perpetual virginity ("Mary ever virgin" in the ancient Confiteor), since the Bible mentions brothers and sisters of Christ (Matt. 12:46; Mark 3:31; Luke 8:19). Furthermore, it states that Joseph did not know (have sexual relations) with Mary "until she had borne a son" (Matt. 1:25).

ANSWER: Hardly any Christians challenge the doctrine of Mary's virginity and the miraculous Virgin Birth of Jesus, because it is clearly detailed in Matthew 1:18-25, it is affirmed by Luke 1:27, it is stated by Mary herself (Luke 1:34), and acknowledged by the archangel Gabriel (Luke 1:35-37). However, a more debated doctrine — the one that you challenge — is that of Mary's *perpetual* virginity. The usual reasons for doubting this teaching are the two objections that you presented.

From the fourth century, almost all great religious teachers (including the three greatest Protestant reformers — Luther, Calvin, and Zwingli) agreed to the statement of the Second Council of Constantinople (A.D. 353) regarding Mary's perpetual virginity. All these brilliant scholars knew that the Greek words for "brothers and sisters" were also used to refer to other close relatives — cousins, nephews, nieces, etc. They also knew that the Greek and Hebrew usage of the word for "until" (as in "until she bore a son") does not necessarily imply a different action after the "until." Jerome cites *many* scriptural examples of this; also the use of "firstborn" whether there were subsequent siblings or not. One ancient author around the time of Christ, wrote of a woman who *died* giving birth to her *firstborn* son. Obviously she would have no children after that child, who was still called "firstborn."

So these two objections (and others) have been answered, or at least neutralized, countless times through the centuries by both Catholic and Protestant Bible scholars, including those who jointly published a book entitled, *Mary in the New Testament* (Paulist Press). The bottom line taken by most scholars is that the perpetuity of Mary's virginity can't be either proved or disproved by Scripture alone. In such situations, the Catholic Church then relies on the other source of revelation — consistent and ancient tradition — to reach its doctrinal conclusion; this back-up reliance on tradition is itself advocated by the Bible, in the eight places cited earlier in this treatise.

Let me briefly list a few of the many reasons for maintaining that the "brothers" of Jesus were related "brethren" — "kinsfolk" (perhaps mostly cousins) — but not siblings of Jesus, not children of the Virgin Mary. Who were his own "brothers" who did not believe him? (John 7:5). Who were those "brothers" asking for him as he preached (Matt. 12:46; Mark 3:31; Luke 8:19)?

These relatives included James and Joseph (or Joses), Simon and Judas (or Juda) as cited in Matthew 13:55 and Mark 6:3. At least two of these, James and Joseph (or Joses), had a mother named Mary, according to Matthew 27:56 and Mark 15:40. But that Mary was certainly not the same as Jesus' mother, as is clear from the context. Significantly too, Mark felt it proper, before naming the "brothers," to describe Jesus, by way of distinction, as the "Son of Mary" (6:3). Whenever he or the other Gospel writers speak of the "brothers" in Mary's company, none, directly or indirectly, relates their birth to her. They seem to be associating with Jesus only during his public ministry.

Nowhere, directly or indirectly, are the "brothers of Jesus" called the sons of Joseph. Rarely, if ever, did a son take his father's name among the Jews — a fact which excludes one of the "brothers" by that name, and thus neither could he have been a son of the Virgin Mary.

There is a remote possibility that the "brothers" of Jesus could have been his step-brothers from a former marriage of Joseph, but this goes counter to a strong and ancient tradition that Joseph too was a lifelong virgin (symbolized in religious art by the lily in his hand).

The Greek word for brother (*adelphos*) means blood brother, but its use in the New Testament is vastly extended to include both near and distant relatives as well as associates. It is not always easy to know which meaning is intended in any given passage. Paul refers to James the Apostle as the Lord's "brother" (Gal. 1:19), and Peter stood up in the midst of the one hundred twenty "brothers" (Acts 1:15), addressing them as "brothers." Jesus "appeared to more than five hundred 'brothers' at one time" (1 Cor. 15:6), and he was "the first-born among many brothers" (Rom. 8:29). Silas is described as "a faithful brother" (1 Pet. 5:12), and Paul speaks of a Christian as "one who bears the name of brother" (1 Cor. 5:11).

Both Hebrew and Aramaic (the native language of Jesus) have no word for cousin, and the Hebrew word *'ah* (brother) is used in the Old Testament for kinsman, translated by the Septuagint as *adelphos*. The Greek has the word *anepsios* for cousin, but the influence of the Septuagint dictated the use of the ambiguous *adelphos*.

Mary is never called the mother of these "brothers" of the Lord. There is no mention of them in the episode of the three-day loss of Jesus at age twelve; yet it would have been unthinkable for a Jewish mother to leave her children at home so that she might travel.

If Mary had other children, they would be younger than Jesus, since she was a virgin at his birth, and he was a "firstborn" child. Such younger sibling children would not be telling Jesus what to do, as his relatives did (Mark 3:20-21; John 7:2-5). Nor would Mary have been consigned to the care of John by Jesus on Calvary (John 19:27) if there were family members who could take care of her.

All of this, and much more circumstantial evidence, leads us to believe that the "brothers and sisters" of Jesus were kinsfolk but not siblings, thus indirectly supporting the ancient tradition of Mary's continued virginity after the birth of Jesus — the prerogative of her "perpetual virginity."

The doctrine of Mary's *perpetual* virginity may not seem important at first, but a closer look shows that it is important to manifest the uniqueness of Mary's place in salvation history. The womb that bore the God Incarnate was appropriately reserved for him alone, and not to be used to bear any other creature. Moreover, by her virginity *irrevocably* dedicated to God, along with her lifelong commitment in marriage and her unmitigated consent to accept the hardships of motherhood, Mary became the one person in history who could portray in combination the three highest human commitments: marriage, virginity, and parenthood. Thus, she was the most unique and the most Godlike of all humans that have flowed from the creative hand of God.

God saw fit to highlight his Son's divinity by a certain exclusivity in certain aspects of his life. For instance, in manifesting his palm-strewn entrance into Jerusalem, Jesus chose to ride on a colt that no one had ever ridden (Luke 19:30); he was laid in a tomb that no one had been laid in (John 19:41). Likewise, he chose the womb of a virgin who had never known man, and who would bear no child but himself. This sacred vessel that bore the Messiah was to be reserved for him alone. Thus, while experiencing the privilege of motherhood, Mary would still remain forever a virgin.

This exclusiveness that characterized Mary's womb as the abode of the divine Messiah was prototyped by the passage in Ezekiel 44:2-3 (referred to in one of the common vespers readings for Marian feasts in the Byzantine liturgy): "This gate shall remain shut, for the Lord, the God of Israel has entered it. The Prince himself is the *only one* who may sit inside the gateway." It is noteworthy that this was the eastern gate that Ezekiel spoke of (verse 1) — the one that led directly to the sanctuary of the temple, for "the glory of the Lord entered the temple through the gate facing east" — "the place of my throne" (43:4 and 7). The God-Man Messiah required exclusive rights to "His throne" — the womb of Mary, pre-figured by the Eastern (Golden) Gate of Jerusalem, which is still closed to this day.

Cognate to the material in this booklet is a two-tape album of audio tapes by Father Hampsch, titled, *Scriptural Basis for Marian Devotion,* along with many more of Father's tapes, videos, books and booklets. It is available from Queenship Publishing Company, P.O. Box 42028, Santa Barbara, California 93140-2028, (800) 647-9882. Cost: $11.95, plus $4.00 shipping and handling.